200

SPEAKING POEMS

speaking poems

by   Ric Masten

Beacon Press   Boston

ACKNOWLEDGMENTS

A number of poems in this book first appeared in the booklets: *Who's Wavin'*, *Sunflowers*, and *Let It Be a Dance*, made available by *Sunflower Ink*, Palo Colorado Canyon, Coast Route 1, Monterey, California 93940.

Woodcuts by Ric Masten

Copyright © 1977 by Ric Masten

Beacon Press books are published under the auspices of the Unitarian Universalist Association

Simultaneous hardcover and paperback editions

Published simultaneously in Canada by Fitzhenry & Whiteside, Limited, Toronto

Printed in the United States of America

(hardcover) 9 8 7 6 5 4 3 2 1
(paperback) 9 8 7 6 5 4 3 2 1

Library of Congress Cataloging in Publication Data

Masten, Ric
    Speaking poems.
    I. Title.
PS3563.A814S6   811'.5'4   76–47034
ISBN 0-8070-6376-2
ISBN 0-8070-6377-0 (pbk)

If the production and launching of this were a kite,
then heartfelt thanks must go to:

Buz and Carol Johnson
for the paper, sticks, and the Snappy Tom glue

Uncle Frank and Aunt Ruth
who have a place for flyers
and a room with a view

Chris Rawson
who had much more than a hand in it

David Fowler and Proctor Academy
who helped me get it off the ground

Dick Dunlop
who believes the thing can fly

and
Billie Barbara Masten
who holds the string
and
      keeps me on this side of the horizon

CONTENTS:

If this book should happen to fall into your hands, my wish would be that you wouldn't read it but rather went out and found someone to read it to you. To sit somewhere in the morning sun or by a window on a rainy afternoon, listening to the sound of this. What follows was meant to be said to you, not read by you and I believe the difference is the difference between feeling and thinking. I do not need your analytical mind stopping to measure the weight of these lines, I need your creative spirit flowing to help me free what the printer has locked up here.

Ric Masten

A university English class, mostly freshmen and sophomores. A smattering of juniors and seniors. A popular course and a popular instructor, true. But a full house in this overstuffed classroom on a warm May morning on the last day of classes?

Up front is a bearded, middle-aged man in faded jeans, preparing to regale the class from a thick notebook of typed sheets extracted from a tattered, bulging, leather bag. He says he's distinguished because he dropped out of five colleges, thought about jumping off a bridge, and came back to life. He writes some words on the blackboard: Birth, Death, and Resurrection. He says he's going to read some poems about them. Initial class reaction — bemused but tolerant.

By the end of some thirty-five minutes, something tremendous has taken place. First, the nodding head snaps up, not quite sure what has happened, hit between the drooping eyes with "a sleeper." The class is suddenly alert. That verbal slap in the face isn't, as it first seems, an offended performer saying, "Wake up, you stupid bastard and listen to *me*." It is a *poem,* and it tells the groggy listener that somebody understands him. Next, "a bell curve" and the realization that something very sympathetic and very close to young ideas is being said in a wonderfully funny, but tremendously effective way. Nobody ever said it like that before. Rapid fire they come: "inventing the wheel." Lots of laughs — but there's some real meaning in there, too. Then, "three for anne sexton" and "buel." Silence; perhaps a murmur or two between seats. A clear and powerful comprehension. The verdict is rushing in. It is decisive. This cat is great. The very greatest.

The push to the front of the room at the end of an hour all too soon elapsed. A deeply felt laying on of hands. One girl clasping through tears that permit only a stammered expression of profound feeling. Another proffering thanks: "I'm graduating this month and this is my last college class. It's the best one I've attended in four years." Deeply moving moments as the class reluctantly disperses.

Ric Masten succeeds, for he quickly, and, I think, permanently touches and grasps something very specially meaningful to the young in a manner few of us have the gifts to do. What's more, he doesn't bring anything particularly new, when you get right down to it. He says: "I've been there; I know how it is; I sympathize; I identify; I'm lonely too." Yet, with his direct and energetic delivery, Ric Masten does reach his listeners, particularly these young adults whose less than twenty years have thoroughly convinced them they have it all figured out, and he can strike instant emotional fire. He's "telling it like it is," but when he's done you *know* he's been there, and you *know* he understands. He's not fooling you and, by god, you're not ever going to fool him.

This volume contains most of the poems Ric Masten read that warm, May morning. What he means when he calls them "speaking poems" is that they aren't intended for reading. They are meant for the hearing. Sure, to see them on the page you can get some of the sense of the qualities of his free and easy verse, so free that punctuation, capitalization, refinements of regular line, foot, meter, and rhyme have little meaning as such, but you don't receive the full impact. Ric Masten is not the poet who wants you to think, to ponder, to analyze. He wants you to listen, to hear it said, to let out the laugh, to swallow the lump, and then go on. It works brilliantly.

These "speaking poems" dwell upon the joys and pains of writing, the paradoxes of the real(?) world (the question mark is his), and the comings and goings of males and females of assorted species.

It's a volume you *can* enjoy alone, and every time I read these poems, I laugh, and gulp, or get all shook up, as the case may be, for the contents herein say a helluva lot, just on the printed pages. Once you hear them spoken though — and the best is by their creator — you'll quickly realize that this poet is emotional and, yes, he's romantic, and yes, he protests, even rages in his way, against those whose idiocies make them kill for Christ, beat the black man down, or commit any number of stupidities in the name of God, mother, or whatever. Nonetheless, it isn't the conventionally emotional, romantic, nor protest poetry you're probably used to. Ric Masten is a true troubador; he isn't out to *sell* you on anything, but he's got something mighty important to tell you. His brief stanzas, most of them, aren't exactly lyric, but they are, in the aggregate, full of soaring lyricism. When you hear them, they do things to you, though you may never be exactly sure just what or how. But you love it.

Jordan Y. Miller
Kingston, Rhode Island

dragonflies

Rather than the usual numbers, I have chosen three creatures to head up the sections of this book. Three living things that symbolize, at least for me, the themes I will be touching on.

Here in this first group of poems, to express the pain and joy of the creative act, I choose the Dragonfly. An insect that spends its life both beneath and above the surface of things. At the bottom, subterranean and grotesque at times, but like the poet and artist splitting his own skin to emerge, rising up winged and iridescent.

i wish i could remember
what i knew when i was five
i think i had the answer then
having just recently arrived

i recall
that i could change into a dragonfly
and when you know how to do this
you know everything

no wonder i cried
when they sent me off
on that first day of school

1. LOOKING FOR PATTERNS

i collect small
typewritten words
and fly them
    looking for patterns

sometimes they rise from me
in clouds
like birds off a field
to circle and then wheel away
for no apparent reason
    and i
lie empty as a pasture
left behind
defined only by these dark fences
of mine

    western civilization
    waiting for the punch line

missing the point

2. A BELL CURVE

if your carpenter
didn't know what batterboards were
you are probably living in a lopsided house
the carpenter's apprentice
will carry and stack a lot of lumber
learning his trade

and when it comes to brain-surgeons
i believe in grades
bell curves and all that
i want to see him flunked out
long before he gets into my head
asking a nurse
what all the funny looking wrinkled stuff is
and god help the electrical engineer
who gets his wires crossed

but how do you grade a poem?

i mean wouldn't it be a little bit
like trying to grade a dream

      ah — student
      your dream started off well enough
      but fell all apart in the middle
      too much sex for sex sake
      and the ending was quite frankly trite
      at best this is a C- dream

parents — faculty — students — friends
what we have here is the finest trade school
in the history of the world
      period
so let's hear it for today's tool and die makers
and leave the dreamers be

3. IDEAS

they strike when least expected
and with each bite a rush of excitement
has me dropping everything
grabbing at the line
to find most often nothing
      there at all
except the feeling of a dream
i know i had but can't recall

i do my fishing on the other side
and if i'm lucky
clean them over here
      like this one
i got yesterday in a restaurant
on a paper napkin that never touched my mouth

it's not much to brag about
      being small
and rather insignificant
but may i say
poet to poet
you should have seen the ones that got away

4. INVENTING THE WHEEL

i don't often read other poets
and i'll tell you why

when i finally get around
to sitting down in the middle of the road
to invent the wheel
having spent days
gathering my materials around me
and having just figured out where to drill
the first hole
it's enough to make you break down and cry
to look up and see
some brilliant young S.O.B.
on a bicycle
        go pedaling by

5. CANNIBAL
(This for all poets
I have carefully avoided.)

i see by the posters
you gave a reading at the forum last night
i didn't forget
i just didn't attend

had the meal tasted as good
as i suspected it would
foolishly
i'd feel diminished
if undigestible
the evening wasted
either way i spared myself what would have been
a miserable ordeal

if you have anything to do with poetry
i think you'll know and understand
how difficult it is
to go and watch someone else serve up
the eucharist
to sit behind a hand and analyze the footwork
holding back petrified
that you'll get out of control
      and eat it up
      and enjoy it

a reformed cannibal
can't be too careful
so i keep myself away from any kind
of plump juicy missionary
and dine alone on my own
      cold potatoes

6. THE CORPORATE WORLD

for someone caught in the paper claw
of a corporate world
the watercolor
hanging in his office
was good enough to be terribly distracting
he had talent alright
enough to keep one small part of his mind
        waving free
like ahab's arm
beckoning from that elusive dream

        but how do you ask an orthodontist
        to take the bands off the kid's teeth
        i mean
        do you go to him and say
        remove the braces dr. bently
        i'm running off to the islands
        to be an artist
        and i can't afford them anymore
        or do you get a pair of pliers
        and do it yourself

the young and romantic
might find this hard to believe
but you simply cannot get to tahiti from here

        damn you gauguin
        and all other white whales

7. TO A LITERARY GIANT
AND OTHER DAREDEVILS

if i acted crazy — forgive me
but i'm a dare devil too
and when i arrived at the jump site
and saw the monstrous crowd pressing around you
i was afraid you might not see my bike

but you gave me a tired smile
and waved from the foot of the ramp
a marvelous feat considering all the distractions

out on the edge a promise
is a dangerous contraption
having little to do with bravery

if you can't say No
your Yes means nothing

and you are much too valuable
to waste on the snake river

8. PUBLISHED AT LAST

on the river there has been a separation
and we don't know where he is
but she
slender as a water weed slipped past
bleeding darkly from the broken place

    appearing
briefly in the rapids
swept along waving bravely
throwing kisses
as only she could do

      we tried to reach her
       but the current was too strong

that was yesterday
her eyes like great
dark stones still weigh
     me down
      beneath the surface
of her much deserved success

9. THREE FOR ANNE SEXTON

1.

your poetry
     is not a pleasant thing
     all sunshine and butterflies
     passing into oblivion
     uneventful
     as a lazy summer afternoon

not at all
     it comes down on me
     the work of a distressed angry bee
     and where it hits me
     does not feel good

your stinger
     stinging me and stinging me
     till my whole being
     swells up with ideas
     painful enough to bring me wide awake

and sometimes
i hate you for it

2.

anne
i suffer the fate of a fan

(June, 1974)

      i read your poems today
      rode them like horses
      magnificent beasts
      and i was impressed with the way
      you've harnessed your pain
          with the way
      you've kept yourself sane
      riding those
              wild
                    twisting
                          dreams
                              down

to a standstill
down to a fanfare
      admiring the way you could trot them around
      under perfect control
      no wonder they gave you
          the prize
      but the photograph on the dust cover
      the cow puncher face
      the big floppy hat
      i could have done without that
      and the terrible hurt in your eyes

(October of the same year)

      and now they tell me
      you've gone down under the hooves
          with sylvia
      anne
      was there ever a dream
          couldn't be rode
          or a dreamer
              couldn't be throwed

3.

        poets
        are a skittish breed of cat
        crouching in the doorway
        we make our presence known
careful
        where we put our feet
we must be

        for there is only one room in the house
        and in it two voices
·   one that shouts
out cat out

the other calling
come kitty
pretty kitty

        there was this over-sensitive siamese
        and she could only hear the anti-voice
        the dark one

and jesus
she described it well
filling books with the pitch
        timber and tone
        the awful sound
that hounded her childhood
ruined her youth
and finally chased her off
to curl up and die alone
out in the garage

        poor pitiful thing
        shouted down
        by a half truth

10. ANOTHER KIND OF NOAH

and yet when my friend marvin
the mad poet comes out of the zoo
every six months
     one shoe on
     one shoe off
i'm always glad to see he isn't cured
that he still limps in his mind
     old nutty marv
because you know i really don't want
to run the instant replay
of yesterday's baseball game
i need his insane rhymes
like straws to clutch at
not the box score — i watch him

     paul gauguin
watching through his own window pain
his crazy friend
     vincent
winding his head up in gauze
knowing the hurt to be the very ground
in which art grows
and far better for him at least
than filling galleries with slick paintings
of wet city streets — colors reflecting
or of little kids with big sad eyes
at fifty bucks a throw

and though it seems unfair of me
i need him there — a crazy man at sea
     adrift
     tending his mad menagerie
     another kind of noah

i need him there — dropping a line
each time i fall
into that awful
     blue period of mine

11. HOW TO PLAY THE BANJO

no
even if i could have
        i would not have
spared van gogh the pain of cutting
        his ear off
and robbed myself of those sunflowers
sorry about that vincent
sorry about that
        myself
and yet
for you who say be totally sensitive
know that i once knew a ditch digger
who bled to death in his own trench
because he could not grow a callus
        couldn't play banjo either
without cutting himself to ribbons
        on the wires

i need my thick skin for protection
otherwise i couldn't say anything
        of consequence
without breaking down completely
right here in front of you
        and you wouldn't want that now
        would you

total sensitivity
        well
it's sort of like an orgasm
you can only stand just so much of it
before you go right out of your gourd

12. THE PRICE YOU PAY FOR SUNFLOWERS
(Song poem, music on pages 87, 88, 89)

you come out of that place again
i gaze into your face again
try to read your eyes again
today
you walked right in and sat awhile
stroked the striped cat awhile
just as tho you'd never been away

and when i asked you how you'd been
you looked up from the cat and then
you sang a song so tender and so strange
closed your eyes and let it come
and when you finally get it sung
you answered
oh — i'm just about the same

sunflowers
time and time again
i need to spend an hour
with my sunflower friend
sunflowers
light the way
put a touch of color
in the long dark day

i offered you a cup of tea
but the way that you looked up at me
i knew you hadn't heard a word
i said
your mind so full of crows in flight
and pinwheel spinning starry nights
and no time in the dream to rest your head

but time is for the ticking clock
and you're between the tick and tock
bleeding from the passion in your brain
so put another bandage on

and sing us all another song
and fill us
with the beauty and the pain

    of sunflowers
    time and time again
    i need to spend an hour
    with my sunflower friends
    sunflowers
    light the way
    put a touch of color
    in the long dark day

the afternoon is dying fast
your songs are bits of flying glass
the colored edges cut into
my eyes
and looking through the salty mist
i saw that you knew how to risk
and father said — all else is a lie

and when you couldn't take no more
you went out through an open door
looking for your blinding field of hay
you left us rich but feeling sad
'cause you were sane and we were mad
but i guess
that's the price you pay

    for sunflowers

13. A MOMENT OF TRUTH

in some other life
i must have been a bull fighter
a little spanish rooster
    hot stuff
    in my suit of lights
but not so hot on sleepless nights
my mind out there in the pens
where the bulls wait like mountains
    dark premonitions
    milling around
    restless
all my brave tomorrows

    hey amigo
    tell me
    is this where
    you really want to be

no not at all

except
in the afternoon
when there is no time to think
and hats are flying thick as crows

except
when i consider doing something
less dangerous for my sunflowers

except
when i parade through the kitchen
with a bleeding ear like this — held high

the fruit of the day
the prize
    and perhaps from you
    a small
    olé

14. PULITZER PRIZE WINNER

of louis simpson i knew nothing
except that he had won the pulitzer prize
for poetry

so when i saw that he also
was visiting the university of michigan
i went to hear him read
        to sit beforehand watching
while other interested students and faculty
trickled in chattering lightly nonchalant

amusing myself by trying to pick
        our prize winner
out of the crowd up front
and while doing this realized
that everyone in the room
was the picture of a poet
        young and flowing
        old and fussy

finally
arriving down the aisle
simpson was there
looking like a certified public accountant

        by the clock
        he took exactly
        one hour of my time

afterward
crunching along
through a crisp ann arbor afternoon
i considered
getting a haircut

15. A SLEEPER

to be a poet reading
is chancy work at best
tough enough to face rejection
but worse
far worse this:

you fell asleep
even as i read you closed your eyes
and dropped your head upon your chest
and to this day i marvel
that you kept your seat
        nodding
        east and west

and although i find it sad
i guess it's only human
that looking back upon a sea
of open faces
i can best recall the one that slept
and wonder
were you overtired
        or simply bored
with all that i expressed

only now writing this
years later
have i thought to ask about the dream
you might have had that day
and all
        i may have missed

16. THE WRITING ON THE WALL

if we show them at all most of us
who write our secrets down and call it poetry
prefer to slip it under the door and run
and if we must be present at the reading
disguise ourselves
      in soto voce and pale monotone

but here was one who could take us
into his personal life and show us around
as if it were a house for sale
exposing everything the way it was
and never once it seemed rushing ahead
to straighten up a room or kick the dirty linen
      underneath a bed

i got my questions ready
how could he do it — and why
it was such private property
and we were total strangers
just in off the street — looking
not necessarily there to buy
but then toward the end of the tour
i realized there was nothing in this place
i hadn't seen before
and when i told him this at the door
he took me by the hand and thanked me
      for helping him feel so at home

outside as we were leaving
i saw where some street philosopher
had taken paint
and sprayed a classic on the wall

      there are no strangers here — it read
      i know myself
      therefore
          i know you all

17. BEFORE MR. HOWARD
COMES ALONG MRS. JAMES

let me say
i have done this long enough to know
    i don't write my poems
    we do
and so i live much like
that indistinct little man in western movies
the one in shirt-sleeve and vest
who seems to exist only at the window
of the telegraph office
    never shot
    never kissed
his reason for being
simply a gimmick to further the plot

    like him
i sit at the end of my pen
    hunched over
sending and receiving
taking the messages down
reading them back to you

    and this just came over the wire

GOOD NEWS STOP EVERY HUMAN RELATIONSHIP
THAT HAS EVER BEEN OR WILL EVER BE ENDS IN
SORROW FOR SOMEONE STOP GOOD NEWS ONLY IF
WE USE THE INFORMATION AND TELL THE PEOPLE
WE LOVE THAT WE LOVE THEM AND DO IT TODAY
STOP TOMORROW IS ONLY A FIGMENT OF OUR
IMAGINATION STOP I LOVE YOU

JESSE

18. AN OLD HUNTER

(for Robinson Jeffers)

i found him reflecting
in his stone tower
               alone
his profile against the window
poet
why so silent in these your latter days
have you nothing more to say?

i was coming on strong — fat
with young ideas
beating the bushes
shooting at everything in sight
he turned his face to mine

         when you have said
         what it is you have to say
         and played all the obvious variations
         you will learn to sit quietly
         in the afternoon
         and listen to the thicket

and thus i left him
just off the trail
an old hunter
waiting for the game
to come to him

         one shell
         left
         in the chamber

19. ON THE MOUNTAIN

somewhere about a third of the way up
he came striding down the trail
and caught me unaware
a poet
staff in hand — naked — thin as a whip
wild gray hair framing the sunstained face
his bright eyes blue holes
                the sky showing through

when he saw me resting there
he laughed out loud
    friend, he said
    i have been to the summit
           and found nothing there
          absolutely nothing
then laughing again
he went on down around the bend
         and left me

with my brand new dayglow knapsack
ten dollar compass — waterproof boots
remembering how i'd sharpened my knife
till it shaved the hair
on the back of my wrist
preparing myself for almost anything but this

still i was young then and it wasn't until i too
had run out of places to climb
         that i began to wonder
where he was going and what he was after
         laughing that way
and so turning around
         i followed on down behind

and if i took you by surprise
this morning coming down the path
believe me i was only laughing at my self
        sitting there

20. WHERE THE POEMS COME FROM
(To an idea of Robert Blys)

it is dark
on the underside of morning
for me it is
and anxiety waits here
a cold blooded reptile
coiled into a sluggish knot
a hunger that keeps the birds away
whispering

                fear
                fear
                fear

                  i retreat
to exorcise with barbara walters
brewing coffee
and while doing this
watch the field from the window
sometimes a three legged fox appears
not every day but when she does
she kills and eats the lizard

and what i was feeling turns around
becoming what it always was

                a tool to use
                a wand to wave

till afternoon and evening vanish
and i can see the voice of a lark
an illusion — true
but one that sheds light on everything
and makes it look so easy

at least till
night descends the capstone under which it all
begins   again.

codfish

When they are landed, codfish must find the space we call reality a hard place to be.

In this section I will verbalize awhile on the real world, or at least the one I think I see. Racially, religiously, conservatively speaking, I view the human dilemma as terribly funny at times. I mean it can be really laughable, unless of course there is something fishy about your sense of humor.

a squirming trophy
delivered rudely
with a slap and a shout
to agonize on the paradox

      one eye down
      on the dark souring wharf
      the other up
      in a towering sky

born
beginning to die
    i am
like a codfish
flopping about
at the edge of all this
    in and out
        of my element

1. LONELINESS
(Song poem, music on pages 90, 91)

standing by a highway
waiting for a ride
a bitter wind is blowing
keeps you cold inside
a line of cars is passing
no one seems to care
you look down at your body
to be sure you are there

sitting in a hotel
staring at the walls
with cracks across the ceiling
and silence in the halls
you open up the window
and turn the TV on
then you go down to the lobby
but everybody's gone

and this is loneliness
the kind that i have known
if you've had times like this
my friend
you're not alone

so you leave the empty city
and go down to the shore
you're aching to discover
what you're looking for
the beaches are deserted
in the morning time
a solitary figure
you walk the water line

you come upon a tidepool
and stand there peering in
and when you touch the water
the circles do begin

they lead to where a seabird
lies crumpled on the sand
so you take a single pebble
and hold it in your hand

    and this is loneliness
another kind i've known
if you've had times like this
    my friend
    you're not alone

you come back up the beaches
at the end of day
and see how all your footprints
have been washed away
no
nothing is forever
we. are born to die
so may i say i love you
before i say goodbye

    i must say i love you
    before i say goodbye

2. THE WAY TO TEACH
*(It isn't so much having a question
to ask, rather the ability to create one)*

and so
he let them have their games
until the tide was fully out
        and when it was
he came upon the rocky beach
a may-pole of a man
among the shouting children
and bending down beside a magic pool
        peering in
he waited
till a ring of faces gathered
at the edge of this attention
then slowly reaching through the mirror
gave a sea anemone
        a punch
who did what sea anemonies will do
quickly folding in
on what should have been a lunch

        WOW!

he said — eyes popping
then abruptly rising
but keeping in mind the length of his legs
moved on up the beach
        the children scrambling behind
        with questions

3. GRANDPARENTS/GRANDCHILDREN

trying hard to understand human nature
i
having pacifist leanings
find my son learning karate
breaking bricks with his bare hands
so that he could kill a man
in two seconds
he says smiling
as i go up the wall

and i
being the son of militant ex-catholic
atheist parents
get myself ordained a minister
much to the disgrace of my old mother
who's reedy voice calls me on the phone

ricky! — she squeaks

as always speaking
like a punch and judy show
and i as always looking
for the alligator to jump up
and hit her with a stick

ricky! — she squawks

you're not gonna let them
put Reverend in front of your name
in the phone book are you?

now
i suppose all this explains
why the grandparents and the grandchildren
usually get along so well

they have a common enemy

4. ENCOUNTER

it was just that i was
very touchy that day
and really that's
all i can say
to explain why
while walking through
the sears & roebuck department store
i happened to get into
this fist fight with a mannequin

5. WITHOUT KITE AND KEY

i can understand the stove
    the bifocal
    and some of the other stuff
but benny
without the kite and the key
what in hell is electricity
and please spare me
    the zero/infinity
    form of energy routine
seeming to this untutored mind
a kind of doctrinal line
demanding a greater leap of faith
than a catholic or a baptist makes

it strikes me . . . (a little electrical
                engineering humor there)

that you
who believe in electricity
should wear a habit and shave your head
to go with the mystical smile that you smile
while seeing the light
pretending you know what goes on

you may be pious enough
to actually own a phillips screwdriver
one of the chosen few
but where is the juice
when the generator shuts down

    like the spirit and soul
    of the dear departed
    where has it gone?

6. MICHELANGELO

high in the scaffolding on his back
michelangelo bites his lip — sighs
and then begins to paint the hand of god
     down

          below
sweeping the chapel floor
a little serf leans his broom against the wall
squints up
and with an arm full of trash
stumbles out through a graceful arch
mumbling to himself

     damn faggots

7. BUEL

i've seen the eyes lookin'
at my beard in the mississippi airport
    i've seen prejudice — hell
i've hid in the men's room — two hours
waiting for my plane — just showin' my feet
    i've seen prejudice — but you're right
i can shave it off
i'll never see those eyes lookin'out from inside
    black skin

buel
have you ever seen a honky and felt anythin'
but anger — maybe envy?
have you ever looked at your black brother
and felt anythin' but pride — maybe shame?
how about guilt
    you ever felt that lookin' at me — i do
    lookin' at you
not because my people did your people over
my people also worked kids to death in the
work house
fed christians to lions — burned witches too
but that was my people — not me
and i ain't gonna hang in my family tree

i'm only guilty of being unable to ignore the
    color of your skin
like i was taught i was supposed to do
when i was a kid and there ain't any way
you could know about this
    being black
    or for me to tell you being
white

but buel
i been lonely
can you understand that?

8. A PLACE FOR CONSERVATIVES

i must admit it bothers me more
than just a little bit
to see an airline pilot with dandruff
sitting around
slightly wrinkled
chewing gum
looking like any one of us
     i mean
when you see the crew
go passing through the gate
don't you want the captain
     to be a tight-lipped man
     with close cropped hair
     eyes like steel doors slammed shut
     crisp white shirt
     slacks creased so sharply
     if you weren't careful
     you could get a nasty cut there

why i'd turn in my boarding pass
just like that
if some freaky long-haired cat
came bopping by
with an earring on one side
saying

     hey baby
     i'm gonna take us for a ride

believe me i'm finally convinced
there really is a place for conservatives
or would you go to a neurosurgeon
who bit his fingernails—
seen knocking his drink over all the time
     i mean
would you really want to do business
with either one of these guys
the morning after

he fought all night with his wife

    not on your life
    not me at least
    if i'm getting on that plane
    going under that knife

what we need here
are hard minded
cold blooded
machine-like people
in a culture as techno-
logically advanced as ours has become
    we cannot all afford to be
    human

9. THE BREAKFAST SPECIAL

a toasted english muffin
with whipped creamy butter
and a steaming mug
of mountain grown coffee
it all sounds so good on the menu
fresh ranch eggs
conjuring up pictures of
mother, father and i on an outing
flying through a summer countryside
in an open tin lizzy
mother holding her floppy hat in the wind
laughing. . . . banjo music playing
and chickens everywhere!   scattering
scurrying back to a barn
full of sunshine cracks and aromatic shadow
where clucking hens nest in secret places
laying eggs for children to find
put into baskets and bring us for breakfast
yes i'll have some of that this morning

pretending i've not
been to the concentration camp
and seen the eyes staring through the wire
and seen the miles and miles
of shopping basket cells
with barely room enough to move or sleep
forgetting how they helplessly stand for days
eating off tin trays
drinking from galvanized tanks
watching their lifes work roll away like teeth

taken out of the circle of things
crispy bacon strips
and country cured ham
have nothing to do with the slaughter

we eat words   and no one says grace
                        and no one gives thanks

10. BURNING TRUTH

the mail comes
and i lose another friend today
to sweet jesus

head bowed
i read the news written in your own hand
somehow antiseptic now
on the cleanest piece of paper
i have ever seen

    praise be to god
    praise god
    over and over and over

you gave the answers
from beginning to end
with no space left
for walking mountain roads again
two men
talking in the twilight
playing with the questions

    god knows
i need a crutch at times
to get this gimpy soul of mine around
but not a burning truth that we must
    kill each other over

11. HOUSE OF GRANDFATHERS

in the house of grandfathers
the dusty old flowers sit around
fishing for smiles
sometimes they read stories to themselves
from torn yellow pages
and it is amusing for awhile
but they know why i come

      it looks like hard work old man
      and no one to lend a hand
      except well meaning girls coming
      like hornets with their stingers
      getting in your way with cylinders — tubes
      and see-through tents

it seems to me if you were home
you'd be done with your labor
and resting already

      i kept the watch awhile but couldn't stay

good-by old man — old dandelion
i wish i were the wind

12. A FARM ACCIDENT YEARS AGO

the horses shied and then wild-eyed
bolted from the field
racing back toward the barn
traces flying
the mower still attached
and running close behind
your father
shouting an alarm
as that ugly snapping arm
reached out
taking everything off at the ankle
weeds and corn and hollyhock
and then in slow motion
sweeping through the stems
of two small boys frozen in surprise

      and sometime later
in a photograph we find
those grinning little peg legged petes
proud as punch
posing
      though the color and shape
      are exactly right
      an aritificial limb
      is what it is
      and can be put on and taken off

      but the story that comes with it

walks
and walks and walks

13. WHALES — OFF PALO COLORADO

today i saw the whales
moving south along the coast
and had to stop the car and get out
and stand there just watching

one of them came in close to shore
and i thought to myself then
that the whole journey would be worth it
just to see the magic of this atlantis — rising
blowing and steaming from the sea — an island
of life
        today i saw the whales and i was healed

i can tell you now of the dancers — the three girls
and the dark wet highway — and the car
that came hurdling into their young lives
and how the rain fell for five days as we followed
slowly behind black limousines — three times
slowly with our lights on

but the sun returned this morning
and the rain has washed the air clean
and brought the ventana mountains in so close
they cut my eyes
        sometimes it hurts to see things clearly

for those girls the dance had just begun
but they went out dancing
trailing veils behind them and somehow
this simple act tells me that they too paused
somewhere along the way and saw
        the whales moving south along the coast
        on a day like today

i hope you will forgive me
for trying to put order and sense to it all
but if i don't can you tell me
        who in hell will?

14. A LOOSE END

it's true i've put off
dealing
    with one aspect of my father's life
    a loose end so to speak
    perhaps because he died when i was so young
    and i remember him not so much as a person
    but more of a presence
        a feeling

so it's not him that i must
finally
    get around to, rather the end of him
    he was forty-nine when he passed away
    i was twelve—and he seemed older than god then
    but now with me at forty-six i can see
        he was in his prime and his
        untimely

death is what really has me
bothered
    the shadow of this event just ahead
    the date crossing my path—an open fracture
    in the shape of a question mark
    i ask myself
    could i ever be older than
        my father?

and a kind of panic
fills me
    to break through the barrier
    and find myself alone on the other side
    without him
    i think i'd rather die first
    and in the next three years if i'm not careful
    this could be the loaded gun that just might
        kill me

15. A SNEAKING SUSPICION

i have given my pets the power
and let my little dog amazing grace
get such a grip on me
that more than once i've folded maps
and called off an extended trip
it becoming more than i can bare
to watch her napping in the sun so unaware
trusting to the moment
oblivious to the desire
        of man and flea

the side of me that lags behind
and drags its feet
gets hold of my imagination
till i have myself confined
in the wire world of the kennel
waiting in canine limbo
brave and stoic
with pricked ears listening
keeping watch on the door
expecting each moment to be the moment
        the master reappears

and i do this to myself
till i must cancel travel plans
deciding not to go
unable to stand the thought
of missing myself so

that
and the sneaking suspicion
that once on the road
i'll forget her as quickly as i
will be replaced by something
        alive and moving in the brush

16. THE ANNUAL CHECK UP

every now and then i discover this
        strange lump
in my abdomen which i finger
when no one is looking to see if
        the soreness
is still there and it always is
and so in fear and trembling i go
to see my doctor and hear
        the bad news
and this kindly old bird hops around me
like a crow with a piece of tin foil
poking and peering
until stroking his chin he declares
that i am in A-1 condition and if i'd stop
handling my pancreas it wouldn't be
        so sore

and yet always in the end
i leave his office with the certain knowledge
that i will be
        dead
in six months the good doctor keeping my
        awful infirmities
from me so that i can enjoy what little time
i have left and bravely with this information
hidden under my coat i return home
to be with my family and together
we climb the hill in back of the house
to sit a spell
and really watch a cloud move

i guess you'd say
i was a bit of a hypochondriac and that's OK
it keeps me close to things
and on this ward we are all
        terminal
anyway

17. THE ALTERNATIVE

imagine
that it wasn't me
you came here to see today
rather the statesman
                comic
                entertainer
                philosopher
                theologian
that you admire the most

the he or she
who has driven a line of words
into your life
        an idea
like the pin into a hinge
and you moved on it

arriving early to assure yourself
of a good seat
you would find tacked to the door
        the small print
stating that it was true
your idol was here
but if you came inside
you would have to remain till the end
of the program
which would last for eternity

                every one of you
                would have turned away
                at the door i believe
                so don't tell me
                you want to live forever

death
will lose its sting
only after
you consider the alternative

18. THE SECOND HALF

i turned forty a while ago
and came dribbling out of the locker room
ready to start the second half
glancing up at the scoreboard
i saw that we were behind
    7 to 84
and it came to me then
    we ain't gonna win
and considering the score
i'm beginning to be damn glad
this particular game ain't gonna go on
    forever

but don't take this to mean i'm ready
for the showers
take it to mean i'm probably gonna play
one helluva second half

i told this to some kids in the court
next to mine and they laughed
but i don't think they understood
    how could they
playing in the first quarter only one point
    behind

19. A KIND OF HOPE

i guess you'd call him a revolutionary
but he laughed real laughter
and when he was quiet his eyes were sad
so i hung around and listened to him talk

he said
      we have broken the ocean beyond repair
      the crabs are leaving
      we will soon follow

he said
      we live in an insane asylum
      where the sensitive must go insane
      that is to say go sane
      and then must kill the pain
      with pill and needle

he said
      the next time the conquering heroes arrive
      the future is gone in a nuclear flash

he said
      and there is no time left for the corn
      to grow

but the fact that he bothered to get out of bed
this morning and say it gives me
      a kind of hope

20. ON BUTTERFLY WINGS

you know for the life of me
i can't recall what happened
last good friday
christmas i can
because mother got smashed
and the baby seeing his image distorted
on the surface of a thousand ornaments
     cried all day
and on easter it rained
so that the candy hidden
in the grass got sticky
and we had to wash the ants off
before we let the kids out but somehow i missed
     good friday

looking the other way i guess
like i do
when i pass someone walking the roadside with an
     empty gas can
muttering under my breath
about the high cost
     of funerals
and how the undertakers are bleeding us dry
     like vampires
not stopping to realize
we can't pay those guys enough to handle
what scares us half to
     death

i mean
if aunt maude bites the bag in my kitchen
your gonna find me outside in the yard waiting
     for some weird cat
to roll up in a long black vehicle
and clean up the mess — cart the problem away
     smiling all the while
oh
i'll stop by the parlor saturday afternoon

check the flowers out
and have a quick look in the box
but then i never was able
to accept a gift graciously
and it's my loss and no doubt the reason
i sit in my own small house drinking coffee
      feeling homesick most of the time

an old guru once told me
that the only thing
we really have to do in this life
      is die
and i think i shall repeat this statement
over and over
a hundred times each night before i
      go to sleep
perhaps if i could bring myself to believe it
i mean really believe it
and remember what happens
      on good friday
i just might come out and find myself
some sunny easter morning
      on butterfly wings
      rising

& frogs

Without all the croaking who would know there was anyone else in the pond, and so a few words about interpersonal communication and the importance of same. And as you wade through here on your way to the " finale " keep in mind that there is a lot more going on between the princess and the frog than mere kisses.

once upon a time
a warty frog
had a princess come along
and kiss it
        nothing happened

but when another frog
hopped up
        something did

and for those of you
wondering what to do
while waiting
for your prince to come
i say
        enjoy the frog

1. MICKEY ROONEY / JUDY GARLAND

with a kind of early mickey rooney
judy garland innocence we go before the church
and state exchanging unspoken trust
for legal documents the soul intent of which
is meant to cover and protect
all moon struck lovers from themselves
when later in the course of human events
comes the expected divorce and property settlement

the magic and excitement traded off
for false security — signed — sealed
and written down — the guarantee
that neither he nor she will ever screw around

and didn't we go down beneath the weight
of that iron bouquet
dead
preserved in the state of wed-LOCK
and is it any wonder that pickled in this
atmosphere
the act of love becomes a habit
like eating in a chinese restaurant
only because it's close and handy
sitting down together with the empty sound
of clicking silverware and nothing left between
but pork chow mein and strained silence
the bill always coming with fortune cookie wisdom
like
> he who catches bus
> will never have to chase it

and other sad commentaries
written by some poor sap and his wife
trapped forever in a cookie factory
on the outskirts of every city and town
in america

2. A SMALL QUIET WAR

and she's at it again — my wife
under the house
digging

i can hear her down there
with my old rusty tools
picking
and shovelling away
hollowing out a place
for her imagination
to run wild in

she's been at it
off and on
for two years now
running back and forth
with one shovel full of dirt
at a time
throwing it into the yard
doing it the hard way
and i must admit i'm always surprised
and a bit annoyed
when i see the size of the pile
she is making
but it's her project
and she says
i'm not and don't have to be
involved

still and all
it has now become impossible
for me
to lie here comfortably
listening to the ball game

3. CONVERSATION

i have just wandered back
into our conversation
and find that you are still rattling on
about something or other
i think i must have been gone at least
twenty minutes
and you never missed me

now this might say something
about my acting ability
or it might say something about
your sensitivity

one thing troubles me though
when it is my turn to rattle on for twenty
minutes which i have been known to do
have you been missing too?

4. COMING AND GOING

i have noticed
that men
somewhere around forty
tend to come in from the field
with a sigh
and removing their coat in the hall
call into the kitchen

> you were right
> grace
> it ain't out there
> just like you've always said

and she
with the children gone at last
breathless
puts her hat on her head

> the hell it ain't

coming and going
they pass
in the doorway

5. ROBERT AND NANCY
(Song poem, music on pages 92, 93)

robert
buried in the tribune with his coffee
reading all about the day before
nancy
just across the table with her teacup
studies what the tea leaves hold in store

    and the now
    the moment slips away
    gone with its joy and sorrow
    he was here yesterday
    and she is coming tomorrow

robert
pictured in the yearbook — mr. football
living in the dear departed past
nancy —
nancy is prophetic — she's a pisces
busy with the yarrow stalks she cast

    and the now
    the moment slips away
    gone with its joy and sorrow
    he was here yesterday
    and she is coming tomorrow

robert
has a photograph of nancy in his office
taken on the day that they were wed
nancy
goes to see a gypsy fortune teller
wants to know what's lying up ahead

    and the now
    the moment slips away
    gone with its joy and sorrow
    he was here yesterday
    and she is coming tomorrow

robert
puts away his toothbrush by the mirror
takes a look and sees his hair is gray
nancy
went to sleep in silence — what a pity
they never really lived at all did they?

      they let the now
      the moment slip away
      gone are the joys and sorrow
      but he was here yesterday
      and she
      was
      coming tomorrow

we live together this way

6. THE HYPOTHETICAL QUESTION

lies beside the road like a stone
and probably should be left entirely alone
it being hypothetical
should we bother with what we uncover
while turning it over?

suppose i should ask you
what you think you would do
if all other humans suddenly vanished
leaving you the last of mankind
and with the knowledge that you are the absolute
end of the line
everything else intact though
      supermarkets — libraries
      gas stations — animals
      everything
just as you'd find it today
      minus people

alone
confronting this situation
do you think you'd commit suicide then and there
without hesitation
or do you think you couldn't do that
but most likely you'd wither away
going out of your mind in a very short time
or are you someone who thinks you could
live your life out combing beaches
      a dog at your side — a stick in your hand
      like robinson crusoe
only this time with no hope of finding
      friday's prints in the sand

in short
how much do you think you need your fellow man?
well
      ask a hypothetical question
      get a hypothetical answer

or so i thought
till i was surprised and brought
down in flames
by a braless young girl
a hard line feminist who took aim and said

    boy —
    if i were the one in the problem you posed
    i would not commit suicide
    comb beaches
    nor would i wither away
    those are the options of a male chauvinist
    pig

    rather
    i would head for the nearest sperm bank
    and being a healthy female
    impregnate myself
    and start it all over again
    thanks to science this time minus
    men

like i said the hypothetical question
lies beside the road like a stone
and probably should be left entirely alone
but turn it over and usually the usual number
    of salamanders — sowbugs
    and centipedes will be uncovered
but look out
for an occasional black widow spider
who kills and devours her mate
a fact
that is not in the least bit hypothetical
and in a funny science fiction sort of way
food for thought

    right fellas?

7. FREE AT LAST

if she's part of the movement
she no longer wants to be a girl
    a chick
    or a broad
    not even a lady
she's a feminist
a liberated woman and i'm for this
a free female
means a free male
free enough to openly express
my childish insecurity

    if a person
wants to whine and whimper
now-a-days a person can
but every time i do
my liberated woman says
    act like a man

8. THE TIME SQUEEZE

is a science fiction film
in which john wayne and betty davis
are contemporaries
but the casting director has kept them apart

for john
the leading lady must be freshened like a drink
a testimonial female
a dream inflated with youth
and though he might act differently
she always leaves him exhausted after a love scene
with no one to talk to
except the gastly remains of ward bond
and gabby hayes

and betty
didn't always cackle that way
forced to play a crazy old crone
once she too had muscle tone and defied gravity
but when a woman's face has been lived in
long enough to have something to say
who would listen
so she makes it up each morning
like a bed
and pays a surgeon to hide the scars

bored with this
the pepsi generation
is out in the lobby buying popcorn
to them it was just another foreign film
they could read the sub-titles
but couldn't understand what they were seeing

and even i
laughed and cried in all the wrong places
till the houselights came up
and i could see
the back of my own hands

9. WAITING

i have in my life tried waiting
in a white room
      for a young working woman
to bring me color
      through a white door

it has been a long morning
with this blank piece of paper
and quiet guitar
the sun came crawling on the floor
and i watched it with no more on my mind
than you
      and this slow
            unwinding
            lonely time

you will come soon for lunch
i will hear your sound in the hall
      your hand on the latch
and then time will fly
      till you're off to work again
      and i am left alone again
washing the afternoon walls
with my eyes
my god
to be a housewife waiting
      always waiting
            and you
            can't create
            while waiting
            you can only
                wait

10. WHITE WATER

i
who had just entered the rapids
of estrangement
was most interested in what she might say
she
who had just come through the white water
the wild water
the mad crazy part of the river

    now tell me
    for the past few years
    have you encouraged your dear spouse
    to get with it
    and find herself
    and be an entity unto herself?
yes
    and did she do it
    i mean go out and find something of value
    aside from the house
    the children
    and you?
yes
    now tell me
    this strange young unexplainable
    new object of your affection
    is she mostly a pool
    for you to reflect upon?

i would hope there is more to it than that
but
well —
yes
    shit
she said

11. STOP ME IF YOU'VE HEARD IT

a story always loses something
in the second telling
and so
   over the years gladys & j. grabowski
developed a relationship
that needed a third party around
to break the silence
   when the children behaved
   the job secure
   if no one had died
   and the car didn't knock
they lived with the sound of the traffic outside
and the clock

   gladys survived
with the jr. league and a brownie troop
and when the kids grew up she went into group
   j. held on playing golf
till his back wouldn't let him
then feeling his age one day
left home and flew to cleveland on business
checking into a motel
as a mr. & mrs. smith
but like the sales pitch says
   after one night in a holiday inn
   you'll not be surprised in the next

in retrospect i think the grabowski affair
was a suicide attempt on something humdrum
and he going to sleep that night
vaguely wondered
if the maid would arrive in time to turn off the gas
   if she did
   perhaps it would be a good omen
if not —
well a story always loses something
in the second telling.

12. WHO'S WAVIN'
(Fragment of a song)

i ain't wavin' babe
i'm drownin' goin' down
in a cold lonely sea
i ain't wavin' babe i'm drownin'
so babe quit wavin' at me

i ain't wavin' babe
i'm drownin' goin' down
right here in front of you
and you're wavin' babe you keep wavin'
hey babe are you drownin' too

oh

13. THE BIXBY BRIDGE INCIDENT

the cup was half empty
the big hand said forty-two past
and the word if there was one
was tired
then suddenly the wind touched my hair
and i became aware of myself
there on the bridge
a weary old bird ready to leap
from the nest and fly blind
to the breathing sea
      below
me
in my best bulky-knit sweater
calmly inching forward
a great sadness
in my blue gray eyes
      hair blowing
      aware now
i paused and listened to the night
for motor sound
and looked for lights
but the world was empty
no one was coming to witness
      my final scene
      the grand finale
and it was such a fantastic
dramatic moment
i decided to come back
and tell you all about it

laughing
shaking my head
i drove home
but it wasn't until i saw the shape
of my own house
that i realized the cup
had been half full
      all the time

P.S.

i was told recently
that of all witnessed suicides
from the golden gate bridge
in san francisco, california
not one
not a single person
has been seen to go off on the ocean side
the horizon side
all
as of this writing
have been seen leaping back
toward the city
and that would be a hell of a thing
to discover half way down

once years ago
i hung by my heels
was swatted — whaaaaah — and decided
to suck air and live
on a bridge near big sur, california
in the summer of '71
i faced the same decision again

    and as i write this
    i realize
    i am
    three months old today

14. THE QUALITY OF LOVE

in the throws of the affair
i was surprised to learn
i could love two women
with intensity
at the same time
one with whom i'd spent many years
and one recently met

now
the quality of these loves
is best described by the difference
in my bathroom behavior — toilet procedure
        at home
though the room was occupied
(my wife in the tub)
when you gotta go
ya gotta go — and i always went
        but in an apartment near chicago
i would carefully close the door
run the water
and turn the fan on

during this time
if a doctor had informed me
i had but six months to live
looking back
i think
i would have chosen
        the apartment
for the first three months
but i know now
i would have wished to go home
to die
        with someone who knows just
        how full of crap
        i really am

15. THE CHICAGO FIRE

No one knows what goes on
behind the faces, for I live in your
golden shadow blinded by a rush of
bright madness, of burning morn-
ing haze, and it is a wonder I
function at all.

Yet here in virginia I wander
down this quiet afternoon with
friends and clearly see the dogwood
exploding in a galaxy of gray
turning green. At my feet tiny
flowers, fern and moss are seen in
perfect detail.

Far from the midwest we walk at
the edge of spring, talking lightly
of things voices in the trees, & no
one knows that i am being con-
sumed by the thought of you.

but now
in another space
      another place and time
i read the above
      curiously
like an old newspaper account
of the chicago fire
having no idea
of what it's really all about

like pain
such things
will not be remembered

16. AFTERNOON TV

unable to get going today i allowed myself
time to lie around the house fallow
watching afternoon TV
and my god i had no idea how awful life could be

. . . there was this young lab technician who
wanted to marry a blind girl not because he loved
her which he didn't but because he had fathered
her first child when she'd been married to his
alcoholic brother

. . . the brother in the meantime had developed
lung cancer while in prison but the surgeon who was
to perform the operation was murdered by the blind
girl's mother who had gone mad after being bitten
by a tropical insect that was part of the young lab
technician's experiments

. . . all this happened when the mother tampered
with these experiments hoping to discredit him so
that her daughter might remarry the alcoholic
brother who had quit drinking and what with the
operation and everything needed all the help he
could get . . .

and i sat there dumbfounded
through a soap commercial and the preview
of tomorrow's ON GOING AGONY
after which i got up and went into the bathroom
with a wrench and in two minutes repaired a faucet
that had been leaking for a year and a half
then resting on the edge of the tub admiring
my handiwork i laughed till i cried

    which all goes to prove
    that there ain't no such thing as a happy
    ending but if you're willing to settle for less
    you can have some real good times along the way

17. THE COUNSELLOR

i was talking to myself again
in front of the mirror
but the glass man only
moved his lips with mine
and said nothing that would help

so i came to you to hear
what it was i had to tell myself
i chose you above everyone else
because i knew
that you would say

       one can
       only
       help oneself

and that is exactly
the kind of smart-ass remark
i will not take
off a mirror

18. THE TOWER

i had a vision once of a tower
here on the shoulder of this mountain
and i became a wildman with a hammer
                    and a dream
but don't be overly impressed
with men who build towers
there are any number of journeyman
carpenters
            and stonemasons
that can tell you how to do it

the building part is easy
it's the living in it that comes hard

with some simple instruction
anyone can hang a door
but if you know the art
of oiling hinges   teach me

19. A NORMAN KING

middle-aged and bored beyond belief
i went into the brush today
and like a child made myself a clearing

with grub hoe and axe
i fought the undergrowth
and did battle with the greasewood and jenesta
the going wasn't easy
the bushes striking — slashing back
until the branches brought me crashing down
a whip-like blow across the face

    thanks
    i needed that

then cursing in childish rage
i rise a norman king
to chop and hack
at the very root of my lethargy

take that
    and that
        and that . . . and
slowly — grudgingly
the enemy falls back
until at last i have myself
a piece of open ground

to rest on — to lie upon
and watch the sky from

    listen the wind is cheering

20. WITH A PIERCED EAR

sitting on United — flight 394
with a pierced ear
i find i have velocity and direction

where i have come from i'm not quite sure
where i am going i do not care

the ticket says philadelphia
i'm not there though
i only know i am somewhere
     filled with this feeling
     and aware of it

strange
how i keep leaving behind
the very thing it is that i'm reaching for
     but then life is for living
     time is a spiral
     and every road
     the road home

look for me
i'm coming

finale

. . . And may all dragonflies, codfish and frogs come to
this —

BIG SUR COUNTRY

it is called big sur country
            where i live
and many men of letters have passed through
none have denied its beauty
but few have
            felt at home here

old henry miller — city born
burned his bald head brown
trying to catch the color of the sun
            at partington

like icarus
            he failed and in the end
retired to a cement maze south of here
more at home in an elevator
than at those
            dizzy heights

and jack kerouac
hitched his way along this granite coast

with no real sense of belonging
        crawling here
        like an ant
he found the place a graveyard
the
  off
     shore
        rocks
        tombstones
        in a ghostly surf
on the road
running like a child in the dark
        hearing things
        in the bushes
he hurried north to hide
in the mulch pits of marin county

and richard brautigan has come and gone
and others
        drawn to and driven off
        by the size and silence of this place

but jeffers knew
        that soaring old predator
        sharp eyed
he knew
        if we could speed
        time up
        fast enough
        we would see
        that the mountains
        are dancing
                and with us

LET IT BE A DANCE

(Song poem, music on pages 94, 95)

let it be a dance we do
may i have this dance with you
through the good times
and the bad times too
let it be a dance

let a dancing song be heard
   play the music say the words
      and fill the sky with sailing birds
      and let it be a dance
     learn to follow learn to lead
  feel the rhythm fill the need
to reap the harvest plant the seed
and let it be a dance

   everybody turn and spin
     let your body learn to bend
       and like a willow with the wind
     let it be a dance
  a child is born the old must die
a time for joy a time to cry
take it as it passes by
    and let it be a dance

    the morning star comes out at night
      without the dark there can be no light
    and if nothing's wrong then nothing's right
  so let it be a dance
let the sun shine let it rain
share the laughter bear the pain
   and round and round we go again
    so let it be a dance

the songs

the price you pay for

Sunflowers

words and music
by
ric masten

you come out of that place — a-gain I gaze in-to your face a-gain try to read your eyes a-gain to-day you walked right in and you sat a while stroked the stri-ped cat a while just as though you'd ne-ver been a-way when i asked you how you'd been you looked up from the cat and then sang a song so ten-der and so strange you closed your eyes and you let it come when you final-ly get it sung you

an-swere oh I'm just a-bout the same sun-flow-ers time and time a-gain you know I need to spend an ho-ur with my sun-flow-er friends sun-flow-ers light the way put a touch of color in the long dark day

I offered you a cup of tea
the way that you looked up at me
I knew you hadn't heard a word
I said
your mind so full of crows in flight
and pinwheel spinning starry nights
and no time in the dream to rest your head

but the time is for the ticking clock
and your between the tick and tock
bleeding from the passion in your brain
so put another bandage on
and sing us all another song
and fill us
with the beauty and the pain

of sunflowers
time and time again
I need to spend an hour
with my sunflower friends
sunflowers
light the way
put a touch of color
in the long dark day

the afternoon is dying fast
your songs are bits of flying glass
the colored edges cut into
my eyes
and looking through the salty mist
I saw that you knew how to risk
and father said – all else is a lie

and when you couldn't take no more
you went out through an open door
looking for your blinding field of hay
you left us rich but feeling sad
cause you were sane and we were mad
but i guess
thats the price you pay

for sunflowers

lonliness

words and music
by
ric mastin

stan-din' by a high-way wait-in' for a ride a bit-ter wind is blow-in' — it keeps you cold in-side a line of cars is pas-sin' no one seems to care you look down at your bo-dy

Chorus: (no chords)

be sure you are there (to 2nd verse) and this is lon-li-ness — the kind that i have known if you've had times like this my friend — you're not — a - lone —

sitting in a hotel staring at the walls
with cracks across the ceiling and silence in the halls
you open up the window and turn the TV on
then you go down to the lobby
but everybodys gone

chorus

so you leave the empty city and go down to the shore
you're aching to discover what you're looking for
the beaches are deserted in the morning time
a solitary figure, you walk the water line

you come upon a tide pool and stand there peering in
and when you touch the water the circles do begin
they lead to where a seabird lies crumpled in the sand
so you take a single pebble and hold it in your hand

chorus

you come back up the beaches at the end of the day
and see how all your footprints have been washed away
no
nothing is forever
we are born to die
so may i say i love you before i say goodbye

i must say i love you
before i say goodbye

Robert and Nancy

words and music
by
ric masten

verse A

Ro-bert bur-ied in the Tri-bune with his cof-fee read-ing all a-bout the day be-fore

Nan-cy just a-cross the ta-ble with her tea-cup she stud-ies what the tea-leaves hold in store

chorus: and the now, the mo-ment slips a-way — gone with its joy and sor-row

he was here yes-ter-day and she is comin' to-mor-row (last time) we live to ge-ther this way

92

robert
pictured in the yearbook – mr football
living in the dear departed past
nancy
nancy is prophetic - she's a pisces
busy with the yarrow stalks she cast

    and the now
    the moment slips away gone with its joy and sorrow
    he was here yesterday and she is coming tomorrow

robert
has a photograph of nancy in his office
taken on the day they were wed
nancy
goes to see the gypsy fortune teller
wants to know whats lying up there ahead

    and the now
    the moment slips away , gone with its joy and sorrow
    he was here yesterday and she is coming tomorrow

robert
puts away his toothbrush by the mirror
takes a look and see that his hair is grey
nancy
went to sleep in silence – what a pity
they never really lived at all did they

    they let the now, the moment slip away
    gone are the joys and sorrow
    but he was here yesterday and she was coming tomorrow

we live together this way

let it be a dance

words and music
by
ric masten

chorus:

let it be a dance we do   may i have this

dance with you?   through the good times and the

bad times too   let it be a   dance, let a dan-cing

song be heard   play the mu-sic   say the words

fill the sky with sail-ing   birds   and

let it be   a   dance let it be a dance   let it be a

dance   learn to fol-low   learn   to   lead

feel   the ry-thm   fill the need to reap the har-vest

plant the seed and   let it be   a   dance

everbody turn and spin
    let your body learn to bend
        and like a willow with the wind
    let it be a dance
  a child is born the old must die
a time for joy a time to cry
take it as it passes by
    and let it be a dance

    the morning star comes out at night
        without the dark there can be no light
        and if nothing's wrong then nothing's right
   so let it be a dance
let the sun shine let it rain
share the laughter bear the pain
    and round and round we go again
        so let it be a dance

Songs published by
Mastensville Music
(BMI)

calligraphy
Rich Hudson

Woodcuts by Ric Masten